PRAISE
BILLY BU

C000131448

"We have become a Soundbite Society! The best way to tackle this insidious trend is to hold up a mirror and let people laugh . . . at themselves. Billy Bullshit is a timely reminder."

—**Herbert Ypma, bestselling author of the HIP Hotel series, photographer**

"If you've been swamped in meaningless corporate-speak and need a good dose of cynical laughter, then this book is just the medicine for you . . ."

—**Andrew Bryant, CSP, global expert on self-leadership, author of *Self-leadership: How to Become a More Successful, Efficient and Effective Leader from the Inside Out***

"Move the needle, shift the paradigm, ideate-proof your business dealings: Billy Bullshit shows you how."

—**Christian Barker, editor and journalist, *The Rake, Forbes Asia, Robb Report, Tatler, Financial Times—How To Spend It, Esquire***

Billy Bullshit Talks Business

by Steve Blakeman and Mike Adams

Published by

◄ köehlerbooks™

210 60th Street
Virginia Beach, VA 23451
800-435-4811
www.koehlerbooks.com

BILLY BULLSH!T TALKS BUSINESS

STEVE BLAKEMAN & MIKE ADAMS

VIRGINIA BEACH
CAPE CHARLES

TABLE OF CONTENTS

FOREWORD

By Tim Reid, BAFTA Award-winning co-writer
of *Peter Kay's Car Share*

I've read this book from cover to cover. What a load of bullshit. You'll love it.

If you've picked this book up, it's probably because you know what a ridiculous amount of codswallop, of jargonistic flimflam and flannel we all talk at work. Yes, all of us. We're all guilty of it. We all drop into the in-talk, the lingo, the acronyms and pseudo-speak that we hope will make us look clever, in the know and on the inside. But wouldn't it be great if we could, as Greg Dyke famously put it at the BBC, cut the bullshit?

And a big first step to getting back to speaking plain English would be to laugh at all the twaddle we talk. So hats off to Steve and Mike for inventing Billy. Seriously, I've never read so much bullshit in my life. So I hope you enjoy Billy as much as I have. He's the business.

INTRODUCTION

Who is Billy Bullshit? Well, he works in the marketing department of Toys R Fun. His official title is "Chief Guru of Imagineering." Given the industry he works in, he shouldn't take himself too seriously. But he does.

Billy talks *exclusively* in bullshit terms. Every word. Every utterance. All total bullshit.

See if you can figure out what he is trying to say. If you can't work it out, then don't worry because we have provided a handy explanation.

Let's face it, we all know someone like our antihero, Billy Bullshit. Every office has got a Billy. Whether it's your boss or a colleague, we can see Billy in someone (everyone?) that we work with. God forbid, you might even see a little bit of Billy in yourself. He is trying so desperately hard to keep up with the latest expressions to make himself come across as being cool and informed. The problem is, he uses so many of these clichéd idioms at work that he has become a parody of himself.

Billy and many others like him are so lacking something substantial in their lives that they feel the compulsion to invent excitement and enrichment in the form of total and utter bullshit. Sound like anyone you know?

You will witness a year in the life of Billy at work in fifty-two recognisable office-based environments as Billy communicates with other team members in sentences entirely constructed from the bullshit words and phrases that we all know so well. Some will make you laugh, others will make you cringe, but they will all make you want to keep reading.

Please join us as Billy navigates through what should be a great year filled with exciting product launches, award wins, press attention and ultimately a promotion but instead rapidly descends into a litany of disasters . . .

1. BILLY BULLSHIT
IN A BRAINSTORMING

TUESDAY 4TH OCTOBER 9.31 AM

I'm happy to dive in here and offer some blue-sky thinking. Straight out of the box, we need to address the elephant in the room. Or is it an 800-pound gorilla? Either way, we are not comparing apples with apples here; it's more like apples with grapefruit. The dipstick research suggests we need to do a deeper dive on the Croc-o-Dial fun phone issues before we can decide on the deliverables. It is what it is for now, but going forward we need to grab the bull by the balls to get us off this burning platform. I don't really know what I want yet, but when I see it, I will know exactly what it is. Come on, it's not rocket science, guys. We just need an overarching, on-trend insight that is a real game changer. A scalable, soup to nuts solution that can market our secret sauce. And if that soup tastes good, then just stop adding ingredients. Am I right? Or am I right?

TRANSLATION: Everyone is talking bollocks (as usual), so I'm going to have to rescue the situation by myself (as usual). There is a big problem here. A very big problem. The Croc-o-Dial fun phone isn't much fun as it appears to have a design flaw—it bites off kids' fingertips. That five-minute Google search you did on the problem isn't sufficient basis to make any informed decisions. You are going to have to do some proper research, which will hopefully stop a full recall. Once you have the right information, you will still need to fabricate a story that the consumer might actually swallow. Oh, and stop overcomplicating it with those useless pie charts that have absolutely nothing to do with the matter in hand.

2. BILLY BULLSHIT
DOES A BRIEFING

WEDNESDAY 12TH OCTOBER 5.01 PM

I have a hard stop in thirty minutes, so let's hit the ground running. It goes without saying that you will be in the trenches on the Urban Terror Wrist development. It's a clusterfuck. Let me paint you a picture. The timeline is tight, there's lots of moving parts, and we need more bang for our buck. You've got to make this sucker pop because we really need to land this one. It's a gilt-edged opportunity to generate some new news and at the same time make you famous. Come on, it's just Marketing 101, chaps. So get started with the pre-planning. There's no time to lose. Put your shoulder to the wheel and don't forget, perfection is the enemy of good. Shoot for the moon, guys, and if you miss, you will still land in the stars. You feel me?

TRANSLATION: I'm leaving here in half an hour whether you like it or not, so stop pissing around, and we can get started. I take great delight in saying that you are going to be working all hours on this nightmare project whilst I will be conspicuously absent for the entire duration. We need a big hit given the Croc-o-Dial fiasco. There is clearly not enough time to complete this complex project, and the client basically wants it done for free. It's an impossible task, which is why I am dangling the carrot of fame and fortune (both are lies as I will take all the credit if it's any good and blame it all on you if it's garbage). Anyway, whatever you produce better demonstrate some originality, but given your collective grade B in Art, that won't be a problem, will it? So get on with it, you lazy bastards, and try to deliver something better than the usual crap you churn out.

3. BILLY BULLSHIT
SENDS AN EMAIL

Hey, Bobby boy, I'm pinging your inbox because our Head of People person has reached out to me to kickstart a dialogue with you following the rather lacklustre sales on the Croc-o-Dial launch, which you were personally responsible for. Let's be candid. I need to circle back and close the loop with you on the cadence of your core competencies. Can I be frank, Bobbo? I know you have been caught up in the weeds, but you don't seem to want to drink from the company fire hose. Our ecosystem dictates that we have to eat our own dog food, but we feel like we are flogging a dead horse with you, Bobsy. Taking the helicopter view, you don't give it 110%. Full disclosure? We really need you to lean in, ladder up and level set. If that's not on-point, then we will need to explore some opportunities for separation as we progress with our ongoing right-sizing of the organisation. I will swing by tomorrow, Bobino, so we can formulate an action plan.

TRANSLATION: Bob, you don't fit in here. No one likes you. Not even the nice lady in HR. And you totally cocked up on the Croc-o-Dial launch. Pack your cardboard boxes because tomorrow is your last day, buddy.

4. BILLY BULLSHIT
ON A CLIENT DINNER

FRIDAY 28TH OCTOBER 11.13 PM

It's great to talk turkey and ring-fence the challenges that we have been facing of late. Irregardless of my best efforts to put a fork in the problems associated with the Croc-o-Dial, it got away from me. My bad. Naturally, I'm the throat to choke. That said, I don't really want to throw anyone else under the bus, but we need to stamp on the heads of a few chickens as a lesson to the rest of the coop. Then we simply need to repurpose the roadmap, rewrite the rulebook and reboot the relationship. And trust me, there won't be a repeat of this shit show, not on my watch. So we lost a few kids' fingertips, but we survive and advance. Worst case scenario? We took some collateral damage and we are where we are, but we live to fight another day. And you are going to really dig our new Urban Terror Wrist toy. It's da bomb. Stickies and smokes?

TRANSLATION: Boy, have we fucked up. Even worse? We got found out. Now I've got to spend a fortune on this dinner with the client whilst I get my arse kicked. Joy. I should have been in control of the situation but frankly had no clue what the hell was going on. It was that idiot Bob. Anyway, he is getting fired tomorrow, which will be a lesson to the other imbeciles in the office. Some loosely based war platitudes along the lines of "what doesn't kill us makes us stronger" and that I will personally take charge of the battalion, blah blah blah. Then order the double Cognacs and a few Havanas. Crisis averted.

5. BILLY BULLSHIT
LEADS AN INTERVIEW

Hola, Rafe. It is really outstanding to connect. And you are looking sick, my friend! So let's get this show on the road. Now, I could extol the virtues of being part of this world-class organisation until the cows come home, but I'm not about to do that, Rafe. I just want to hear all about you. As a centre of excellence, we get to cherry-pick the cream of the crop. We expect our thought leaders to hit it out of the ballpark, go full throttle and smash it into the nanosphere. End of. Look, we need a digital ninja. If not a digital prophet. A visionary, if you will. And without fear of contradiction, let me tell you that if you work smarter rather than harder, then one day you might be able to climb the greasy pole and reach the heady heights of "Chief Guru of Imagineering" just like yours truly, developing cutting-edge toys like the new Urban Terror Wrist. So, do you have the right stuff, Rafe? You got the chops? If so, you could soon be living the dream. Just like moi. Comprende?

TRANSLATION: Christ, not another limp dick straight out of college to interview. And with a stupid name, a ridiculous top knot and embarrassing bum-fluff beard. (My grandma had a better goatee than that dude.) Anyway, I don't want to listen to a word you've got to say. So guess what? I'm going to do all the talking. And I like the sound of my own voice. Yeah, baby. Oh, and I've got zero intention of offering you a job, either. That slot is going to the cute girl in the short skirt I interviewed yesterday. So what I'm going to do is make you feel (in equal measure) both jealous and inferior about how much I have achieved in my career. Now that's what I call entertainment. Boom.

6. BILLY BULLSHIT
ON A CONFERENCE CALL

FRIDAY 11TH NOVEMBER 4.17 PM

Who is running point on this call, guys? Bob, are you on? I know Jill is dialling in, but she keeps getting kicked out. I'm at the Four Seasons in Koh Samui, but the 4G is a bit spotty, so I may have to dial back in. I'm halfway up a frigging palm tree just to get two bars, for Christ's sake. First World problems, right? Anyway, I need to cascade some intel to you all, but I'm time poor and have limited bandwidth so am just gonna say it. I'm cognisant that we need to close the loop

"The 4G is a bit spotty. I'm half way up a frigging palm tree just to get two bars for Christ's sake" *on Project Urban Terror Wrist before we reach critical mass. You still there? Ok, I thought the call had dropped. Right, then, as I was saying, by taking an entirely holistic approach, we can land this plane whilst we figure out what the known unknowns actually are. I'm not saying we throw the baby out with the bathwater, but we need to take it to the next level. Joined-up thinking is the only way to go to ensure that we dial this sucker up to eleven. Can you hear me? I'm losing you. Hello? Hello? Ah, fuck it . . .*

TRANSLATION: Conference calls are the bane of my life. Why should I have to do them when I'm on holiday? Still, I'm going to unsubtly let you know that I'm in Thailand just to piss you off. I should be there dealing with this project, but as it's half term and I wanted a week in the sun, the kids are in club all day and I'm doing sod all apart from taking pictures of everything and boast-posting them daily across all my social feeds. Anyway, by using the word *holistic*, what I actually mean is that you are responsible for everything whilst I'm away, which, in turn, means that if it goes wrong, you are entirely to blame and I'm Teflon.

7. BILLY BULLSHIT
ON A CORPORATE AWAY DAY

WEDNESDAY 16TH NOVEMBER 7.48 AM

I know this is a big ask, but to ensure best-in-breed collaboration we need to wrap our collective brains around this big, hairy, audacious target. We need to think about this away day in terms of the gestalt because the whole is greater than the sum of its parts. We need to ensure that we stay the course to maximise our human capital and focus on not trying to fix what isn't already broken. Sense check—it won't be a cakewalk, but it's no guts, no glory. The good news is that you are all match fit, and the chemistry in the team is intoxicating. You just need to own it to drive it and seize the day to ensure that we have joined-up thinking. There are lessons to be learned about the difficult Croc-o-Dial launch, so let's get to work and make sure that you eat the elephant one bite at a time. From that, we need a Jean Claude Van Damme good idea for the Urban Terror Wrist venture, and you are the MVPs to achieve that. Don't ever forget you are the next wave, our movers and shakers, our team "Two-Dot-Oh." Just do what you do so well, put in a shift and go deliver. Let me spell it out for you: TEAM—Together. Everyone. Achieves. More. Give me a righteous hallelujah to that.

TRANSLATION: The task we have set on this two-day management jolly is so far out of your collective reach that it's pretty pointless even trying. We may as well have given the brief on "How to Achieve World Peace" or "Why Do We Exist?" The trick here is to shower you in compliments so that you feel all warm and fuzzy, which will then at least keep you awake during the day and out of the bar until 6 PM.

8. BILLY BULLSHIT
CONDUCTS A PERFORMANCE REVIEW

MONDAY 21ST NOVEMBER 10.31 AM

So let's get the proverbial ball rolling on your performance assessment, Danny. As you are aware, Danno, it's a full 360-degree interrogation of your key skills to ensure continuous improvement in your personal KPIs. Oh Danny boy, we are seeking accretive gains in the four key quartiles of your scorecard whilst paying particular attention to your EQ ratings rather than IQ levels. At this time, Dannbo, we are seeing some marginal gains across several metrics, but there are some pivotal learnings to be made. The feedback from your compatriots is very telling. They say you treat them like mushrooms—you keep them in the dark and treat them like shit. That's probably water off a duck's back to you, Dandini, but if you want my two cents' worth, then we need to nip it in the bud. After all, our people are our greatest asset. In my humble opinion you need to start walking the floors and get some more skin in the game with the troops. With these new rules of engagement in place I can see your return on involvement improving hand over fist.

TRANSLATION: Here we are again, the mandatory annual evaluation where we both pretend that it has absolutely nothing to do with whether you get a pay rise or not when we both know full well that's exactly what it means. You think that you also get to appraise me during this process, but the real reason why they call it a 360-degree evaluation is because you basically end up back where you originally started. Anyway, your team despises you because you never speak to them and you lock yourself away in your office so that you don't have to face them. Not that I really care you understand, but it gives me an opportunity to slag you off and at the same time use it as a reason not to increase your salary.

9. BILLY BULLSHIT
REPORTS THE QUARTERLY NUMBERS

On the surface Q3 looks like negative growth, but let's step back, rewind the clock to this time last year and sanity check our thinking around the market forces at play here. If we look at the net-net figure, we have runway for hypergrowth in Q4. Consider this, gents and ladies. With the polenization of both our product pipeline and our new sales go-to-market, I can't see how we can't galvanise a touchdown Q4. After all, the numbers don't lie. The rest is just gravy, right? Am I right? Right.

TRANSLATION: Q3 was a shocker. I know this. Actually, everyone knows this. That fucking Croc-o-Dial problem just won't go away. Last count, 119 stupid kids have lost varying pieces of various fingers. Can't they read the instructions on the packaging, FFS? So, what I am going to do is try and deflect the current problem and redirect everyone's focus onto future revenues with a combination of total bullshit and a dash of blind hope. Will I succeed? Probably not, but if I sound confident enough, a few of the more mentally challenged might buy it.

10. BILLY BULLSHIT
RUNS A SALES MEETING

WEDNESDAY 7TH DECEMBER 2.16 PM

I just want to put a stake in the ground here and talk about the snafu last month. We set the stretch target on the Croc-o-Dial sales to really bubble it up, but the numbers don't lie. It was just an epic fail of even more epic proportions. You are only as good as last week. When you unpack it, we are where we are, but we need to get this puppy back on track pronto. We need some quick wins, so let's get back into the war room because we are building this plane as we fly it. Tell me, what is the strongest arrow in your quiver? Where do we draw the line in the sand? Come on, give it up because time is money, people. Tick tock grandfather clock. Work smarter, not harder. Give it gangbusters, goose it up, grasp the nettle, go the whole hog and give it that extra mile. Give me the FMF. Remember, teamwork dreamwork. Kapish?

TRANSLATION: So, it's become entirely clear now that the ridiculous sales target we set for the Croc-o-Dial at the beginning of the year was never going to be achievable. And if any more kids lose more fingers, thumbs or nails with that fucking toy, then it's only going to get worse. I need to start beating the sales team into submission because it's my cock on the block if this continues to go wrong, and I have absolutely no idea how to get out of the huge hole we are now in. Now more than ever I need the fuck-me factor, or it's going to end up more like the fucked-me factor.

11. BILLY BULLSHIT
AT THE OFFICE CHRISTMAS PARTY

FRIDAY 16TH DECEMBER 11.42 PM

What do you mean you fancy Linda from accounts? Seriously, you can put lipstick on a pig and all that. Or, keeping it festive, you can roll a turd in glitter, but it's still a piece of shit. For fuck's sake, she is properly FULLAB. Everyone knows she is the office bike, and I have it on good authority that the collars and cuffs don't match. Well, it's your funeral, buddy. Be my guest if you want to try your luck and take a test drive, but I'd blaze a trail tout de suite if I were you because it looks like the hired help is truffling around. And that's the kind of input that isn't welcome. Linda also looks like she might be up for it, so you might have to jump through a few hoops and do a little grunt work before you can saddle up. It's not like it's your first rodeo though, cowboy. We've both been on this merry-go-round ride a few times before. Come on, pick up the slack, play the game and open the kimono so we can get this party started.

TRANSLATION: Actually, I shagged Linda at the Xmas bash two years ago. I haven't been able to shake the memory ever since and have spent more of my time trying to avoid her. I mean, FULLAB (Fat, Ugly, Looks Like A Boy) is not my usual type, but it was lean pickings at the time. Anyway, I don't want anyone to know about it; otherwise, my reputation as a ladies' man will take a bit of a hammering. So if I can get this excuse for a human being to get jiggy with it, he can hopefully take the spotlight away from me, but he needs to get in there before the bloke handing out the canapés sticks his tongue down her throat.

12. BILLY BULLSHIT
PULLS A SICKIE

MONDAY 19TH DECEMBER 7.02 AM

Briony, listen, here's the headline. I will give you the body copy later. I'm not coming in today. I've picked up the lurgy from that fucking prick Deric. I mean, seriously, why come into the office when you've got man-flu and infect the rest of us? Now everyone is dropping like flies and out of action for the high stakes game. It feels like I've been gargling with gravel and someone has stuck a red-

hot poker up my arse. Just my buzzard luck, too, because I've got that boondoggle in my schedule over at the golf club with Nige from Big Toy Box. You know me, though; I'm never off sick, I've always been a trooper, and so I will be back with my nose to the grindstone asap if not even sooner. Keep the plates spinning whilst I'm away, put my stack on the back burner, and come hell or high water I will see you bright eyed and bushy tailed tomorrow.

TRANSLATION: I simply couldn't be bothered coming into the office today. Truth is I'm still recovering from the Christmas party. Note to self: must stop drinking tequila and Red Bull. Anyway, I can blame it on Deric, who spent most of Friday sniffling into a Kleenex. I never intended to play golf with Nige. What a tool. And he's a complete bandit. Plus, he will just keep banging on about how many unsold units of the Croc-o-Dial they have in their warehouses. So I'm going to pull the duvet over my head and watch some Judge Judy whilst you lot slog your guts out for the day in the full knowledge that I will be back at my desk tomorrow because there was nothing wrong with me in the first place.

13. BILLY BULLSHIT
PUBLISHES AN ARTICLE

WEDNESDAY 28TH DECEMBER 1.39 PM

Contributor Column, *The Business Times*, London:
When Execution Lets Down Strategy

*Concomitantly aspiring executives, while rudimentary
in their thinking, can sometimes, or more often, lead
the company to head into turmoil around the execution
capability of its people.*

*Microscopic dissection of the facts opens the kimono
against the long-range, telescopic strategy—and reveals
the brilliance of its ineptness. Such ineptitude challenges
the very sandbox of the company's existence. Pain points
acutely put through the pressure test of organisational
DNA are disrupting the ecosystem paradigm.*

*A pivot, now essential, is the only play. A race to the
bottom is the only outcome if a digital shift is not embraced.
With this as the core fabric, the only question remaining*

is how will an "org" quantum-leap their scalability and optimise their human capital effectiveness?

Leadership and diversity are both central to the success of effective execution. While not bound together in unison, neither are they not. But they are synergistic when combined and a powerful force driving the company towards strategic imperatives.

By Billy Bullshit,
Contributor

TRANSLATION: I have absolutely no idea what any of this means, but it sounds like I do. Doesn't really matter, though. It's the Christmas edition, so no one will read it, so I can pretty much write whatever I want.

GIVES THE TEAM A NEW YEAR PEP TALK

MONDAY 2ND JANUARY 9.01 AM

Get listening, guys. Let's get going, get to the bottom of the problem, get busy, get with it, get our arms around it, get at it, get into it, get over it, get under it or get around it, get cracking, get it off the ground, get the hang of it, get weaving, get it over a barrel, get the fuck in, get boots on the ground, get traction, get disrupting, get to the point, get buy in, get into bed with, get the fuck out, get the last laugh and get gone. Oh, and Get Carter. Get it? Got it? Good.

TRANSLATION: Get on with it.

15. BILLY BULLSHIT
WELCOMES A NEW RECRUIT

MONDAY 9TH JANUARY 9.32 AM

Happy New Year and welcome to the club, Natasha! Can I call you Tash? No? Ok. Anyway, my name is Billy, and I will be personally responsible for the entire onboarding process. I'm here to help you climb the mountain in order to empower you and provide the platform you need to succeed. There is no glass ceiling here, and it is entirely non-hierarchical, so essentially what I am saying is I can help you get up that proverbial greasy pole with the benefit of my vast experience. I'm a straight talker, no execubabble, zero bullshit kind of guy who is simply here to help you hit the ground running. Human capital is our number one priority, and you will find some genuinely exciting and rewarding people to work with here. We have some real fun initiatives like Dress Down

Friday when you can wear jeans to the office. I know, cool, right? Then there is Mankini Mondays, Tank Top Tuesdays, Wear What You Want Wednesdays and Thong Thursdays. Seriously, this place is a laugh a minute. You look a little scared, Tash. Sorry, Tashker. Don't be worried. I can promise you that we don't bite—well, not much, anyway. Haha!

TRANSLATION: Right, get your best fake smile in place, Billy. Another two hours of my life that I won't get back whilst I onboard another wage slave. Onboarding? It's more like waterboarding if you ask me. Truth is, I know I say I'm a straight talker, but I'm not. I absolutely love execubabble, and I'm a total bullshit kind of guy. So in fact the polar opposite of reality. And to cap it all, I'm going to try and sell you the pathetic attempt the board came up with to try and create some kind of positive ecosystem in the office. The big idea? Some totally fucking stupid ideas on how we should dress in the office each day. Which nobody pays any attention to. You look freaked out. Probably won't last the week.

16. BILLY BULLSHIT
REVIEWS A PRESENTATION

So, who owns this deck? Dominic? But I delegated it to Cristian. Anyhoo, I thought we were just crafting it, but it's still 329 charts, guys. This is death by Powerpoint. Come on, less is more. Don't sell me the sausage. I just want the sizzle. Jeez, I'm not sure if we are singing off the same hymn sheet here. Let me put you in the picture. We are T-minus two days and counting until the big enchilada from Big Toy Box drops by with his entourage, and you showers of shit are still blueboxing. The fat lady hasn't started singing just yet, but she's just coughed up a big ball of phlegm into a tissue. Look, I want you to cherry-pick the best bits about the Urban Terror Wrist and cut the fat off the meat. I know we are facing a strong headwind after the Croc-o-Dial shitfest, but I need you to go full throttle to get us back on the happy path. I want to know if this thing can scale. Scalability is this month's watchword, and it goes without saying that failure is not an option.

TRANSLATION: None of you douchebags ever listen to me. I gave this one to Cristian because I knew he would cock it up and that would give me some ammunition to fire his sorry ass. I have no clue as to whether the deck is actually any good because I lost the will to live after reading just eleven charts, so the best feedback I can offer is that the presentation is too long. The fact that the client meeting is only scheduled to be forty-five minutes should have been a clue, and don't give me any of that crap about some of the charts are just dividers. I read something on Forbes about scale and scalability and it sounded pretty good, so I decided to use both of the words here. Sound good, don't they? The only thing is I'm not quite sure I'm using them in the right context. No matter. If I don't know, then these brain turds will have absolutely no clue.

17. BILLY BULLSHIT
RUNS A TOWN HALL

TUESDAY 24TH JANUARY 12.07 PM

Welcome, welcome and thrice welcome. Come in closer, everyone. I don't bite. Often. Well, not at work, if you know what I mean? Wink wink, hey, ohhhh! You were there! Haha, ok. Come on, now; settle down, chaps and chapesses.

Let me first start by saying that this past three months we have been wrestling the negative press problem on the Croc-o-Dial to the ground. Truth be told, it's been a tad problematic. But congrats to Sandra and her team and the rest of the war room for weaponising our strategy. We really kicked that issue in the guts. Huge congrats. Kudos. With a capital C. I know that sometimes it's simply easier to let some fires burn, right? But you didn't. You stuck to the task in hand, and that's a sign of huge cohones, Sandra. Seriously, well done.

Next, the figures. Last quarter has taken a marked uptick from Q3. The runway and pipeline velocity picked up steam, and the sales guys did an epic job of stemming the slippage. Now, if we can get that to hit the triple bottom line, then we all walk away winners.

Lastly, I want to highlight the editorial piece that was featured in the prestigious Christmas edition of Business Times, *penned by yours truly. It has been heralded as equalling, if not surpassing, the writing of Peter Drucker, but I am not one to boast. Suffice to say that you should all read it and think about it in terms of the whole cake rather than a combination of its ingredients.*

Ok thanks, folks. Now, who wants a bite from moi . . . ? Hahaha, oh stop.

TRANSLATION: I am the right person (probably the only person) to run these town halls. A perfect blend of humour and smarts. I get the common people, the Sandras and the Brians of this company—yeah, sure, they did an "ok" job, but I big them up, I lift them, I inspire them. In honesty, though, the main point of today's meeting was to get them to read my article in the *Business Times* . . . it was generationally ahead in its proposition . . . they need to hear that message. Heck, some of them need to tattoo it onto themselves as a constant reminder. Clarity and hard hitting. That's me. God, I am good.

CHATS TO THE NEW RECEPTIONIST

WEDNESDAY 1ST FEBRUARY 5.32 PM

Hey there—it's Christina, isn't it? Yeah well, I thought that I would shimmy over here to break the ice and introduce yours truly. Bottom line? You are quite the talk of the water cooler and the word of mouse on email! Anyway, you are no doubt wondering who I am? I'm guessing you probably saw me in the town hall meeting last week when I was entertaining the troops. Oh, you didn't see that? Well, that's a pity because I smashed it. Out of the park. Home run. So, I thought I would touch base to see how you are settling in. The other school kids treating you nicely? A word to the wise, if you have any problems whatsoever, then my door is always open. I carry a lot of gravitas around these here parts. Look, as much as I hate to tear myself away, I must fly as I've got a high line dialogue with the big cheese in five, but I wanted to check on your avails for an out-of-office rendezvous ce soir? Not free, huh? Ok, let's just put that idea in the parking lot for now and we can revisit it later. Ciao for now.

TRANSLATION: Even though I am punching well above my weight, I'm going to make all my best moves. It's all about confidence. The chicks just can't resist a guy who loves himself. I know she isn't showing it, but I can tell that she was super impressed when I presented the new campaign in reception. She tried to act disinterested, but I could tell that she was just acting it. Even when she affected that little yawn. Cute. And if she isn't free tonight, that's ok. I will just keep on asking. I love it when they play hard to get. Persistence always pays off in the end.

19. BILLY BULLSHIT
ASKS FOR A PAY RISE

THURSDAY 9TH FEBRUARY 7.39 PM

Can I be frank with you, Chief? It's time to reassess my value to the company and have a powwow about upgrading my package. Despite having a full plate and having to steer a course around some of the deadwood, sales have gone into the stratosphere, and yet I don't believe I am reaping the rewards, boss. You receiving what I'm broadcasting? Now, here is the thing; I see the likes of Bob swinging the lead, and yet he's driving around in that brand-new Toyota Prius. I'm not being funny, but that isn't tracking well with me. Given my compelling backstory, I should be commanding top dollar. Give it a little time to percolate, share it with the top brass, and then we can loop back around on the matter later this arvo?

TRANSLATION: I am absolutely not being funny. I know that I am worth way more to this company than I am being paid, and I'm not getting shafted any longer. Since I've been running marketing, sales have at least plateaued, and that's a big improvement over my predecessor. Well, a slight improvement is more accurate, maybe, but it's still an improvement. I have at least given the boss something to think about with my fifteen-point PPT on why I deserve a new company car, five more days holiday a year and a 20% pay rise. The boss did say that he was prepared to give me all that, plus he would let me work just four days a week as well. I asked him if he was joking. He said that he was but that I had started it. Am still not sure what he meant by that.

20. BILLY BULLSHIT
WORKS ON A NEW BUSINESS PITCH

THURSDAY 16TH FEBRUARY 8.19 AM

I intend to lead from the front on the Urban Terror Wrist project, and my core strategy is to target the low-hanging fruit. I know we did this last year on the Croc-o-Dial, but I want to do the same again, but this time I want to make it bigger. I've seen the brain dump from the previous campaign and have done a knowledge transfer of the key insights to top management, who have rubber-stamped this exciting new initiative. We need a laser-like focus on the key deliverables because this isn't going to happen automagically. You need to ask yourselves one question: are we set up to win? I want you to think like a start-up. Think niche. Think new normal. Let's be that long pole in the tent. Can I be honest with you? We have a chasm to cross, and we are going to have to get granular to get traction. I will give you the air cover you need whilst we divide and conquer, so let's hold hands together on this. I've never been more convinced that together, we can move the needle.

TRANSLATION: Do you recall the really basic new business pitch that I led about a year ago? Well, we are going to do the same exact thing again but call it something different and pretend it's innovative thinking, and somehow that will actually make it work this time. I also love "cut and shut" words, and although the splicing of "automatic" and "magically" means absolutely nothing, it sounds splendid. And anyway, I sold it to the CEO over a few drinks last night and he liked it, so, as far as I am concerned, it works for me.

AT THE LGBTQ+
COUNCIL MEETING

WEDNESDAY 22ND FEBRUARY 10.06 AM

Leo, Leo, come over here, mate. I have been volunteered for this meeting. No clue what it's about. What does LGBT mean? There are some right characters here, eh? Just having a good scope around. Blimey, check out the chairman at 3 o'clock. Camp as a row of tents. Oh, right, we are starting . . .

May I interrupt? Too late. Forgive me, but as I have started, I'd like to finish. Ok, so I want to engineer our thinking around something for a moment. When we say "enterprise-wide diversity," are we trying to boil the ocean? I mean, it's a bit of stretch, right? Speaking from experience, it's gonna be hard to push it deep into these management assholes. They don't bend over and simply take to new ideas on their knees. I am just saying that you guys and girls are going to have to suck it up, that's all.

I know these guys; they are all joined up like some corporate boys' club, you know, all jumping in the bath together after the match. You feel me, Gavin? It's a cock-fest in the boardroom, everyone comparing who has the biggest swinging dick. I mean, Gav, do you want a piece of that? Of course you don't.

And, Mary, some great ideas, but way too ambitious. I know you were just trying to put your finger in the proverbial dyke, but it ain't working for me. You may need to take a haircut on a few of those plans. Oh, I see you already did . . . haha. Just some humour to lighten the load.

Ok, sorry to back up on you, Mr. Chairman, but I have to go and stroke some management cock. Typical, eh?

TRANSLATION: Who are those guys? Never seen them in my life. Way off the pace with their ideas. Embarrassing, really. Not sure if they are straight shooters or not. Hmmm, left me feeling a bit queer if I am honest. Oh well, I won't be parking my butt in that group again.

22. BILLY BULLSHIT
MEETS WITH PROCUREMENT

As you can see from the RFI response, our project investment summary clearly demonstrates how we have pulled the reins in to ensure the price point has been whipped. The proof of concept is undeniably viable, and as a consequence our recalibrated offering is incredibly robust. We have refactored our pricing bearing in mind the current market status and found previously unearthed efficiencies to add additional value. In a nutshell, we have squeezed the pips, sweated the assets, crunched the numbers and sharpened our knives to sense check every conceivable variable to provide what we believe to be an unbelievably compelling future-proofed offer.

TRANSLATION: We found out what our competitors were offering. Then we undercut it. End of story.

23. BILLY BULLSHIT
WORKS FROM HOME

THURSDAY 9TH MARCH 7.01 AM

I won't be around to help herd the cats today as I'm diving headfirst into a PPT due for the KOLs at ToyCon '19 next week in Dubai. I'm contactable via mail but off limits for voice. I'm heads down on this hot potato so I can get in front of the game, and I need some downtime to square the circle on the needful for this preso. I'm not going to lie to you, I need a light bulb experience to make sure it cuts the mustard, but it feels like I'm trying to nail jelly to the wall right now. I need some divine inspiration, and the office environment is not conducive to getting my creative juices flowing. I need to jump into the thought shower, lift and shift some learnings and make it happen. Net net, I'm going to be offline for the duration, flying under the radar, off piste and OOO, so if you need to pass the baton, then you will have to issue a hospital pass.

TRANSLATION: Working from home is simple code for hanging around in my PJs all day, no shower or shave and resembling a bag lady (and smelling like one too). Frankly I just couldn't be arsed with getting up, or the tedium of the commute or listening to the rest of the team talk drivel whilst I am trying to finish this presentation for next week's conference. Truth is I have pretty much finished it (well, I mean copied most of it from a presentation I found on Slideshare), so I can complete that on the flight over there. So I will pretend I need to have some time away from the office, whereas I will be mainly playing FIFA on the Playstation

MEETS A PROSPECT ON A PLANE

SATURDAY 18TH MARCH 1.13 AM

David? Is that you? Well, bounce my bollocks, it is you! Fantastic. I have been meaning to get some face time with you, and this Emirates onboard bar is "da bomb"! Well, not literally. Sorry, folks, relax; it's only a turn of phrase.

So, Big D, the D man, where are you heading? My bad. You will be off to ToyCon '19, right? I'm doing the keynote this year. Anyway, enough of me. How's the fiscal been for you? Let me tell you that we have really taken off this year, worked hard on the value prop, if you know what I am saying. Croc-o-Dial was a humongous success, and the new Urban Terror Wrist will kill it. Seriously, guys, calm down. It's just a toy, chill out. Hey, Mr. Sky Marshall, just put the cuffs away. Now, if we can just get the landing gear to work as it should, we can land this bird into record growth . . . did you see what I did there?!

Now listen, pal, you and I are cut from the same cloth, and we see eye to eye. So let's get some time in the diary, press some flesh and carve us out some go-forward momentum, eh? I will have our people connect and schedule a stand up. Oh, you fancy a walk? I'll walk with you. Let me just grab another glass of this rather exceptional Margaux.

TRANSLATION: I have been trying to get some time with him for ages. I think he is impressed with me now, though . . . we speak the same language and, hey, we fly the same way. I am a man who does business on a plane. That's just the way I roll.

25. BILLY BULLSHIT
GIVES A CONFERENCE KEYNOTE SPEECH

MONDAY 20TH MARCH 9.03 AM

Thanks, everyone. Thanks. Is this on? Can you hear me? Yes? Testing 1, 2, 3. Sound guys, are we good? That's a yes? Thumbs-up. Good. Let's get this show on the road.

Now then, to start with, I am going to ask you a question. And that question is, how many of you hate your job? Be honest, now, any of you? One of you? Wow. And do you all lie about other things too? Hahaha, just a joke.

Ok, let's switch gears. Let's talk about disruption.

Some key facts to digest:

Digital innovation will change or eliminate 15% of current jobs in the next ten years—does this mean your job?

Technology advancements in the fields of robotics and AI will fundamentally and irrevocably eradicate some industry sectors—is your sector heading towards a train wreck?

And statistically, when people were polled about their desired job, 4% expressed a desire to work in the adult film industry . . . hahaha, you know who you are! But I jest. Or do I? Who knows? Well, not me.

But here is the reality, folks. Our industry is under threat. The world is changing, and the question for you, my friends, is will you embrace change also?

As I look out across this room, I see a mix of industry leaders and some emerging new entrants. I also see legacy thinkers and dinosaurs of old. I am going to say it as it is: some of you will be extinct very soon, and that's good news for the rest of us, right? Hahaha . . .

I urge you, as we journey our way through this event and over the next two days, to embrace change—think about how you will disrupt your own paradigm and pivot to new iterations . . . perhaps some of you will push into new and exciting technologies and others look for a new career altogether . . . I hear there is a shortage of new talent in the porn industry . . . hahahahahahahahhahah . . . ok, enough.

Please enjoy ToyCon 2019, and don't forget to buy me a drink at the free bar later this evening.

TRANSLATION: Think of me as an Elon Musk or a Steve Jobs. Here to revolutionise the industry. I mean, come on, some of these execs predate the dinosaurs and yet are blind to the impending and inevitable "digital" meteorite about to make them extinct. Perhaps I will have jolted some of the deadwood free to drift off into the oncoming current. Fuck 'em. Move out the way, Grandpa; earthmover Billy is here. Hey, you can't beat honesty. I would bet my last dollar I will either be headhunted or promoted, possibly both, after *that* performance!

26. BILLY BULLSHIT
MEETS WITH THE PR TEAM

WEDNESDAY 29TH MARCH 3.29 PM

We need to create a sense of urgency for the Urban Terror Wrist product launch, so I have decided that we are going to produce a viral video to target millennials. We brought in a subject matter expert, and she has provided us with some killer qualitative insights into the target audience. The really mind-blowing thing is that these millennials are apparently really into sharing both short and long-form content across their various social platforms and feeds. They are gramming, snapping, tweeting and booking like there is no tomorrow! If we can tap into this innate source of virality and harness its power, then we will have a slam-dunk launch which will cost next to nothing and make us all rock stars. Where I'm coming from is that we create a disruptive guerrilla marketing campaign that will connect with our audience to bolster the buzz. Mini fist pumps all round. Get in!

TRANSLATION: I don't even know what a millennial is, but everyone keeps talking about them, so I think we should target them. The SME in question is my niece (who is a millennial herself, apparently), and she should know a lot about them, so I have cast her as an expert. And she is cheap. Am not quite sure what gramming is. Or snapping. I have twittered (twattered?) a few times, though, and have got nine followers now. Anyway, I hear this social media stuff is basically free if it goes viral. Like a virus, I think, so, like, lots of people will get it, but it doesn't make them sick. Or something like that. Anyway, the board understands it less than I do, so I will just tell them it's a "data-driven people-based marketing campaign which is incredibly cost effective," and that should do it.

27. BILLY BULLSHIT
ANSWERS A CUSTOMER COMPLAINT

TUESDAY 4TH APRIL 8.43 PM

Dear Mrs. Bamford, firstly let me pass on my sincere gratitude for bringing this matter to my attention. It is only the valued feedback that we receive from our loyal clientele which enables us to constantly evaluate and upgrade our products and services. I know it must have been incredibly distressing for your daughter to lose her fingernail whilst playing with our new Croc-o-Dial fun phone (which incidentally was our number one–selling pre-teen toy last Christmas), but I can assure you that the incidence of such incidents has been statistically very low. It is our belief that the customer is always right, and as such we are prepared to offer a full refund voucher to spend on any of our market-leading pre-teen range (not including sale items), which should give us closure on the matter.

TRANSLATION: I genuinely don't have any sympathy for your stupid child losing half her finger, nor do I care for the other 322 moronic kids who have done the same in the past month. We sold almost half a million Croc-o-Dials last quarter, so I reckon the loss of 323 infant digits is an acceptable loss. Anyway, you ain't getting your money back, so here is a free voucher that expires in a week's time that you won't be able to spend even if you wanted to because it's January and everything is in the sale right now. Winner winner, chicken dinner.

28. BILLY BULLSHIT
BRIEFS AN ONLINE CAMPAIGN

THURSDAY 13TH APRIL 11.59 AM

Now, I'm no digital native, but I want a real step change in our next social media campaign where we focus on chasing eyeballs for the Urban Terror Wrist launch. I want to drive significantly more traffic to our website so that we get more clicks than a chatty dolphin. We have to push the programmatic piece because after doing a deep dive on the big data that's in our DMP, I am of the firm opinion that we can use that smart data to develop more dynamic creative, which can then be optimised to target our in-market consumers on a one-to-one basis. We can then build an agile platform from which we can micro-attribute our content, which, by the bye, we can use to retarget other similar profiles. That's the beaconicity I'm searching for, and we need to immediately double-click on that strategery. Next steps are to build me an outline straw man or a wireframe, whichever you feel will get us closer to the end point quickest, and let's see if we can make this pass the piss test.

TRANSLATION: I have absolutely no idea what I am talking about apart from the fact that I've been told that no one visits our website, so we need to do something about it. So I Googled some expressions to do with social media and patched them all together to turn it into a verbal brief. I love Google; it makes you an expert in anything instantly.

29. BILLY BULLSHIT
DOES A RADIO INTERVIEW

SUNDAY 22ND APRIL 5.34 AM

If I am hearing you correctly, what I think you are saying is that across the piece the unprecedented development of our revamped range is unequivocally the standout achievement in the marketplace in quarter three. Let me add some colour to that statement. Bottom line, we were back to the drawing board and took a brave business decision to go to the mattresses. We circled the wagons, gathered the brain trust and set sail in our thought canoe. In essence, we delegated the deliverables, acknowledged the key drivers and downloaded the dipstick research. It was then just a matter of bringing home the bacon by empowering our people, laying down a marker with our competitors and incenting every member of the team to look for the white space. Simply put, it was our think-do attitude that was the key enabler here and that really upped the ante. My advice to other marketers? Well, there are always going to be winners and losers in every game, but I would say that for me it's as easy as ABC . . . always be closing.

TRANSLATION: Is anyone even listening to this? It's 5:35 AM and the *Barrie Talks Local Business* slot isn't exactly *Hard Talk* on CNN. Still, it's free airtime. Must remember to throw in the occasional *Godfather* reference to make me look like I mean business. Then, as the segment is called "Drivers & Deliverables," I obviously need to say those buzzwords and to cap it off with an uplifting and suitably generic rabble-rousing quote that I copied and pasted into my head from Sir Richard Branson's LinkedIn profile. Job done.

30. BILLY BULLSHIT
TALKS TO THE IT DEPARTMENT

Long story short, Marvin, I was syncing my smartphone to my laptop so that I had a backup, and now there is a ghost in the machine. It's either some kind of bug or I've been hacked because they have both gone belly up and I'm now running blind, which is situation unacceptable. These are the tools of my trade, and I need them weaponised and fully functioning. The interface is glitching on both screens, and I need to jump on a call with New York. Our CEO is breathing down my neck and I am about to lose the plot. It's your job to sort this out asap, so I want you to look under the hood and leave no stone unturned whilst tracking down the solution. It's probably because you haven't updated the latest security patches on the firewall. And don't waste my time with all the usual technobabble iGod bollocks; this should be meat and potatoes for you guys, so pop that in your mental microwave and see how it defrosts. You on my wavelength, or do I need to draw you a picture?

TRANSLATION: These IT folks, some of them can't even wash, let alone fix a computer. Still, I've been dicking around with my technology, and as usual I've broken it. It's highly possibly that it was something to do with that dodgy website I was looking at on that sales trip last Thursday. I knew I shouldn't have used the webcam. Anyway, I will tough it out and blame it all on IT. I've read *Computing for Dummies*, and I know all the right expressions so they can't talk down to me. And anyway, I'm sure that weirdo Marvin is a serial killer. Or even worse, he's into comic books, Star Wars and World of Warcraft.

31. BILLY BULLSHIT
RANTS AT THE INTERN

WEDNESDAY 3RD MAY 6.17 PM

Henry, with the utmost respect, you are a total fucking imbecile. If you were even marginally less intelligent than you actually are, then we would have to water you once a day. Whereas some people have delusions of grandeur, you appear to have delusions of adequacy. Playing the devil's avocado for a second, it's become abundantly clear to everyone that you are like a fish trying to ride a bicycle, running around like a ferret on speed, dropping grenades in fishponds. When the rest of us are focusing on the doughnut, you are preoccupied with the hole, always barking up the wrong tree and trying to stab the seal with a banana. You have almost singlehandedly derailed the Urban Terror Wrist project and made it FUBAR. And you evidently don't learn from your mistakes. You constantly cock up, and then it's just a case of wash, rinse and repeat. It's like trying to knit fog with you half the time, so I suggest you wise up and grow a pair before we have to cut the umbilical cord, which would be most unfun for us both.

TRANSLATION: This guy is so wet behind the ears he should have gills. He brings a whole new level to total incompetence. I mean, even a broken clock is right twice a day. I wonder if he has a pulse because I don't think any blood is getting to his brain. Too many college nights on the bong or playing beer pong if you ask me. Anyway, this project is now so Fucked Up Beyond All Recognition that it's beginning to resemble a salvage mission. I think it's time to cut the ties with this deadwood, and although it won't be a lot of fun for him, I think I might actually have some sport terminating the twerp.

32. BILLY BULLSHIT
GIVES A PRESS STATEMENT

FRIDAY 12TH MAY 12.17 PM

Best in breed sums us up, Fiona. You know, we built this puppy from the ground up, and it shows. We are envisioneers, disruptors, evangelisers of innovation, enablers and future-casters. Everyone else is trying their damnedest to simply keep up, but they are just lost in our wake. We take a simple product and forklift that concept to new heights. And that, Fiona, that is precisely what we have done with our new Urban Terror Wrist product range. Are you catching what I am throwing? Good. It's all about the team, Fiona. I wish I could take the credit for it, for all of the thoughtware, the bluebox thinking, the ideation, but I can't. Not for all of it, anyway. Most of it, maybe, but not all of it.

TRANSLATION: I am clearly carrying this company forward, and while I insist it's about the team, it's all largely about my total brilliance, which enables me to see around corners and create market-leading products.

33. BILLY BULLSHIT
ON A GOLF DAY

SATURDAY 20TH MAY 1.09 PM

Ah, Mr. CEO, the 'Millard' looks like we are playing this round together! Gives us a good chance to chitchat about the biz. Listen, I read the annual shareholder letter. A real hole in one, eh? Ha, yeah ... classic.

And if I may continue with the golfing analogies, I would like to share some of my thoughts with you. I am concerned we are handicapped by our thinking. You know, we are struggling through the back nine, and some of the players are keeping us in the rough. There's a huge fairway to drive through, and yet some of our client team seem to be using a putter when a one-wood is needed.

So here is a thought. Let's sand trap the limp wristers. Just full on bury them in a bunker. For the ones who have a promising swing, get them some time in the driving range to hone their skills. I think Dan is a wonderful coach to help lift their game. Now, our scratch players, our real pros, I think we add some pressure. Par for the course is not good enough for them. They should be scoring under par. The elite top 1%, the likes of you and I, well, we chip in with the prize money and spend the tour in the nineteenth hole. Feel me?

Right, let me play this shot. Fuck. Shanked it. Ah, it's heading towards the car park. Oooh, that's not your car, is it Tim?

TRANSLATION: The CEO loves talking about our people. He says they are our best asset. And I agree, except for when they are shit, of course. I totally charmed him with my golfing metaphors and also put forward a really solid strategy around talent management. Sometimes some serious brownnosing is needed if you want to climb the ladder. Fucking wish I hadn't hit his car with that tee shot, though . . .

34. BILLY BULLSHIT
CLOSES THE SALE

TUESDAY 23RD MAY 3.06 PM

Can I just interject? Let's talk brass tacks. Firstly, that was a great presentation, Charlie, and, guys, thank you for sharing your objectives. It's clear from my perspective that this is a slam dunk. Now, I know you have some reservations about moving forward, so let's agree to disagree on that, but my advice is that you don't want to win that argument, Jeff. Don't get stuck in the weeds. Let's stick a pin in that for now and loop around to the executionables once you have had a good chance to kick our tyres. After all, the only way to test our metal is by working with us, right? Ok, next steps: let's journey-line the terms, make sure we are joined up in our thinking and ink this thing! Yeah? Come on, Jeff, lean on the pen. Let's do this!

TRANSLATION: I fucking nailed that deal. Closed. I will be amazed if that contract is not signed. Once again I come to the rescue of our woeful sales department, plus I used some super advanced sales lingo to shut down any objections and fuck them up against the wall. Billy one, sales zero. Coffee is for closers. And mine is a double shot macchiato to go . . . whoosh!

35. BILLY BULLSHIT
IN A PRODUCT REVIEW MEETING

Team, let's pull the reins in on this new iteration. Just pump the brakes on this whole deal. Being positive, I really love the whole camouflage theme, and the level of realism on the gun is spot on, but for now I want to put this on the back burner. Given the current climate, I have a few mild reservations that a mock pistol and knife kit called the Urban Terror Wrist is going to fly. Let's pool our resources, pick up the slack, push the envelope and really pressure test our thinking. This is not an exercise in pencil whipping; this is about pre-planning, productization, pivoting, pole position propagation. Dig deep, pick your brains and pretty this whole thing up. Because right now selling this is like trying to push spaghetti uphill. Yeah, you know what I am talking about.

TRANSLATION: Holy Mother of Christ, this product is either brilliant or shit. I can't make up my mind. I need a hit product to make the whole Croc-o-Dial recall just disappear. This might be a bit of a risk, but if we can make it work, then I'm solid gold. But if it goes wrong . . . Jesus, what am I thinking about? Of course it won't go wrong. Will it?

36. BILLY BULLSHIT
IS INTERVIEWED ON THE BUSINESS NEWS

MONDAY 5TH JUNE 8.06 AM

BN: *Billy, what is your leadership philosophy?*

BB: *My philosophy in business, and in life for that matter, comes down to six little words—"let's do it again but bigger!" I have been described as a force of nature, an innovator, game changer and market disruptor, so I can't help but bring my A-game to work each and every day. As a business leader I insist that the team always put the "extra" in extraordinary. We go beyond our limits. We block and tackle our way to results, always have. Yeah sure, it can get hairy always moving the needle to new dials, and we often build it as we fly it, but that's business appetite, and let's just say we are always hungry!*

BN: *This is an age of disruption. How are you leading your organisation through these uncertain times?*

BB: *In these cut-and-thrust times, a leader such as myself needs to be VUCA-esque—sorry, that stands for Volatility, Uncertainty, Complexity and Ambiguity. Predictable leadership went out with the dinosaurs. Perhaps we need to date more than we get married. Throw out the rule book, colour outside of the lines, freak people out, jolt the status quo. If we can cascade that thinking across the management team, we will thrive in the face of uncertainty. And in no way is that just management speak. We, I, live and breathe that ethos 24/7.*

BN: *In volatile times, surely a leader needs to be steady, stalwart, and strong to calm the storm?*

BB: *That's nebulous . . .*

BN: *Erm, right . . . thanks, Billy, for those . . .*

BB: *Not at all—sorry to cut across you; it's been a real pleasure being part of the crew. And a sincere and heartfelt congratulations for running such a strong editorial piece showcasing industry icons and the pressing need for strong leadership.*

TRANSLATION: Such weak journalism. Thank heavens I was there to carry that segment. Embarrassing lack of real life and business smarts from their side. I expected more. Lucky I am on hand to impart some gritty perspective. It baffles me how some people have jobs. And yet at least it reminds me why I am at the heady heights of success that I am . . .

37. BILLY BULLSHIT
BUMPS INTO AN EX-COLLEAGUE

THURSDAY 15TH JUNE 9.14 AM

Hey, buddy, how's it hanging? Fancy bumping into you! Long time no see. Well, here's the thing, fella. I've been up to my naked screaming eyeballs in an avalanche of work. We've been future-casting some new product lines, so I've been burning an excess of midnight oil, matey boy. Feature creep has been slowing us down, but we've navigated our way through the chop, and we are accelerating towards the end game at a rate of knots now. It's just a case of ironing out some of the creases, making sure the numbers are fluid and getting the foils ready for the weekly WIP. You know how it is, El Capitano—just living the dream! Anyway, enough of talking shop and the usual blah blah. I really need to press on, but seriously, we should do dinner sometime. Get the families together over a weekend and throw a few shrimps on the new barbie smoker. Let's set that up. Get your people to call my people, and we will get that in the old diary. Laters, dude. Don't be a stranger.

TRANSLATION: Oh Christ, I've been trying to avoid this annoying twat for weeks, but now I've got nowhere to hide. Obviously I need to pretend that I like him (which I don't) and also tell him how busy I have been (which I haven't). Just keep ladling on the familiarities so he really thinks that he is a friend of mine (which he isn't). Now make an excuse to get away from him as soon as possible by throwing him a fake invite to come over for a weekend barbeque with his whining wife and execrable offspring, although clearly I have absolutely no intention whatsoever of following through. And please, in the future, just be a stranger.

38. BILLY BULLSHIT
FIRES SOMEONE

FRIDAY 23RD JUNE 5.36 PM

Anthony, Tony, Toners. Please take a seat. Look, I'm going to get straight to the point; I'm afraid I am going to be the bearer of bad news today. For you, though; not necessarily for us. Anyhoo, listen, Toners, in today's world, business demands more. To put it more bluntly, there is no such thing as a free lunch. The throughput from your department is frankly piss poor, and the whole Croc-o-

*Dial debacle was the straw that broke the camel's back.
Don't get me wrong—we really love you, Toto, but as the
old adage goes, "If you love someone, set them free." I know
that this is a bitter pill to swallow, and in fact we have all
sat in the same seat that you are in. Well, actually, I never
have been, but still, I feel your pain, brother; I really do.
We could go back and forth as to the reasons why, but in
all honesty, Tone Loc, if I agreed with you, then we would
both be wrong. I want to sincerely thank you for your truly
excellent contribution, but the ship is sailing, my friend,
and you have a one-way ticket to your next port. How
exciting for you. I wish I was in your boat. Ok, over to the
people person who will take it from here, Tonester. I have
to get to an offsite. Happy trails, mon frere.*

TRANSLATION: The Tone Man. Nice enough guy, but his
sell-by date expired a looooong time ago. I will miss him.
Actually, I won't.

ACCEPTS AN INDUSTRY AWARD

SATURDAY 1ST JULY 9.47 PM

Well, what a humbling moment this is. I am genuinely humbled to be up here accepting this award on behalf of my talented team. I'm emotional and somewhat overwhelmed and, as I said, totally humbled. Climbing this mountain has been a humbling exercise of doing more with less.

Stripping out the distraction and keeping laser focused on the prize. We were tempted to start trying to fix what wasn't broken, but we stayed true, set our bearing to true north, and here we are today. Literally, better than all of our peers, and that of course means all of you out there. Woah, what a feeling. Being a winner is such a humbling experience. I have said it before and I will say it again: we are in the business of winning, and our business is winning. So, I humbly say to you, fuck yeah, baby!

TRANSLATION: Of course we won this bloody award! The rest of the industry is full of wankers using convoluted waffle in their marketing for what are vastly inferior products. Fuck these guys. Fuck 'em all. Humble? Humble my ass—let's just tell it as it is. Fact is we won, they lost. Now, where is the bar? I'm gonna get shitfaced and rub everyone's nose in it.

40. BILLY BULLSHIT
GETS RID OF A SUPPLIER

WEDNESDAY 5TH JULY 11.02 AM

Chris, every year, we in the senior management OPCO team perform what we call a "Key Record And Partner Profit Executive Review." Or the KRAPPER, for short. It's where we look at our roster of suppliers and assess which ones we believe have long-term growth potential and those who have grass growing on them. It's a rigorous procedure which allows us to make some bulletproof decisions on who we get into bed with going forward. Essentially it allows us to future-proof our relationships. Now, Chris, after a thorough investigation into our business relationship we feel that Planet Friendly Plastics no longer fits the bill for us as your market positioning doesn't reflect the Corporate and Social Responsibility charter we have recently adopted. Consequently, we will be terminating our contract with you and appointing one of your competitors. Rest assured that any outstanding invoices will be settled in accordance with the ninety days payment period outlined in the MOU. So before the dust settles let's clear the decks and bid each other au revoir.

TRANSLATION: We haven't got a new CSR charter at all. Frankly we don't give a shit about the environment. It suited us that you claim to manufacture environment-friendly plastics, but we both know that's a pile of shit because there is no such thing. Don't forget I've visited your factory in Islamabad, and that place chucks out more contaminants than a fake diesel emissions test. Actually, the real reason I'm getting rid of you is that my mate Roland has just become the CEO of Cleaner Greener Plastics, so I'm going to give him the business instead. Oh, and even though I promised you that we would clear all our invoices, we are going to sit on those for at least two years without paying them and will only stump up the cash when we get the letter from the courts. Nice bit of interest to be had there.

LOSES HIS SHIT WITH THE CLIENT SERVICES TEAM

THURSDAY 13TH JULY 4.12 PM

Fuck, fuck, fuck, fuck, FUCK! What in cocking hell do you fuckwits think you are doing?? The Big Toy Box is one of our biggest frigging clients and you guys, in your infinite fucking wisdom, think it's a good idea to exclude them from our client retreat and, for the love of Christ, think it's ok to double charge them for something that we haven't even fucking designed for them yet, let alone delivered to them. The Urban Terror Wrist hasn't even made it to beta-testing yet and may never even hit the shelves if we don't pull our finger out. Not only that, but they still have over 2,000 SKUs of the Croc-o-Dial in their warehouses that they can't shift, and we ain't doing a sale or return deal. Seriously, what planet are you wank-stains from?! Planet Fuck-Stick-Dick-For-Brains, that's what planet!

TRANSLATION: I am pretty sure at least one of them broke into tears when I left the room. Good. GOOD! Epic fail on their part, and I am sorry, but I am done pussyfooting around these clowns. Some of them couldn't think their way out of a paper bag. Well, we know one thing is for certain—they won't make *that* mistake again, and I am very certain that their respect for me just went into the stratosphere. Yeah, I would be surprised if I get anything but total compliance and collaboration moving forward. Mind you, it has been postulated that the client team gets absorbed into my group. I must admit, I would probably do a better job than the current manager despite me effectively doing two jobs. Onwards to save the day somewhere else . . .

41. BILLY BULLSHIT
RECEIVES A HR COMPLAINT

TUESDAY 18TH JULY 9.01 AM

Samantha, seriously? Are you on crack? Someone in Client Services has said I swear too much? Well, they can just go and fuck themselves sideways. That's fucking bullshit. Tell them to man the fuck up and not be such a bunch of flaccid cocks. Total bunch of twats, each and every one of them. I am taking this all the way up the cocking ladder, Samso, so let's see whose head rolls after I socialise this. The tail doesn't wag the dog on my watch, Sammy. This is not my first rodeo dealing with incompetence and skulduggery, and no one has the right to blemish my personal brand.

TRANSLATION: Are you fucking kidding me? Moi? They complained about moi? Those fucking fuck-sticks. Right, that's it. HR and the whole client team can go fuck themselves. Let's see what the CEO has to say about this . . .

43. BILLY BULLSHIT
MENTORS A GRADUATE

THURSDAY 27TH JULY 12.14 PM

It's Emily, isn't it? Nice shoes, lady. Right, Emo, you don't know what you don't know. So let me brain dump some key phrases that you need to master in order to survive the corporate jungle. If someone asks you if your report is ready, always answer by saying "It's 99% done. Just validating some of the numbers; they don't look right and I know you don't want me handing you inaccurate data."— Emmy, this buys you time to go and start the report. Saved my skin a number of times.

Here is a biggie. When you are in a blueboxing session make sure you bring your thoughtware with you. Never be unprepared. Chip in, ideate, but if you are left up shit creek without a paddle and find yourself drowning for inspiration, step back, 10,000ft view, and think like a start-up. Failing that, do what I do, and say something like "I particularly like Donald's idea, but I wonder if we fly it through the Iteration Cycle whether the 2.0 version might be even more bleeding edge." That works every time.

And whatever you do, don't get caught zero tasking. That's a real brown paper bag job. It pays to get into bed with the winner, Emz. You could do worse than hanging onto my shirt tails if you know what I mean. Catch you on the other side, if not before. By the way, how old are you?

TRANSLATION: If I were a few years younger, I would have a run at her. Wowser, she is cute. Actually, I still reckon I will have a crack. The younger ones love the power trip. I think I struck the perfect balance between flirty and fun and professional. She will go far. I mean, she looked as thick as two short planks, but she has the "assets" to succeed. I might try and reassign her to my project team. Hmmm, seems like the new receptionist, Christina, has cooled off a bit anyway. Actually, she never really warmed up.

44. BILLY BULLSHIT
APOLOGISES

So, Megan, Megsy, Megs . . . this is a bit awkward. Listen, I know I escalated my comms the other day with your team. I don't want to go over old ground—let's not beat the issue to death or dig up the bones, but I do want to say that despite my, er . . . "style" . . . the message was on point, no? Can you see the wood for the trees on this one? Can you parry what I am jousting, haha? Yeah? No? Listen, you will get there; give it some breathing space. My language was colourful, I know that, and I also know that for some people, that directness can be confronting. But hey, I can't apologise for being a force for good, right, haha? I am an "earth-mover." I make shit happen, and if I am not wrong, I think we all ended up in the right place after our meeting. I know you had some resignations, but we always have to cut the wheat from the chaff. We found our keystones, our foundation blocks, right? Look what we achieved through this. Personally, this is a big win, I think, for everyone. Thanks, Meg. I am happy we cleared that little mess up. Fuck it, eh?! Ha . . . . .

TRANSLATION: I simply will not apologise for who I am. Besides, they fucked up, plain and simple. Megan will be fine with this. She just needs to take a chill pill. I am confident this will blow over and we will be better off for it . . . is her name Megan or Meghna? Oh, whatevs.

45. BILLY BULLSHIT
SPEAKS TO A HEADHUNTER

Warwick, I feel we need to refactor the candidate brief. Maybe, just maybe, we need to slow down to speed up. So let me just rain down a thought shower on you, and then we can unpack it and fashion my thoughts into outputs afterwards, ok? Awesome.

So try and keep up; we need a mover and shaker, a Dan Marino quarterback-type guy, someone who is not afraid to take a punt and drive the ball upfield. A collaborator, a team player, a corporate assassin, someone who is not afraid to take some names and equally take no prisoners. Ruthless in execution and yet understands that leaders lead from behind. Someone who can become part of the fabric of our company. Someone motivated to climb their career Everest. Now, that may mean that you need to find the need behind the need or, if not, in front of the need. We need someone who needs the need and will really dig into the weeds and uncover who they really are behind the façade.

They need to be a right-hand man or woman. Can pitch and catch. Challenge conventional thinking and be a change agent. Firm grasp of the numbers and be a people person, you know? I have a strict "no-dickhead-policy," so don't put a wise-ass candidate in front of me who thinks they have already arrived.

TRANSLATION: Just find another me.

46. BILLY BULLSHIT
NEGOTIATES WITH A NEW PARTNER

Roland, the initial quote is way too high. Plain and simple. Sharpen your pencil, dude; you need to slice and dice the figures as much as you can. Listen, my numbers are fluid, and yours need to be too. We are on the same side of the table here. Believe me, we both want the same thing . . . you want me to buy and I want to buy, but the numbers have to soar. It has to be a classic win-win. Sure, I have some risk appetite, but my nuts are in the vice if I sign off on this figure as it currently stands. We got rid of Earth Friendly Plastics to get Cleaner Greener Plastics on board, so don't dick me about. We are all fighting for share of wallet in this market, but do whatever you need to do at your end, and frankly you might need to rein in the squirrels so that we can focus on the imperatives. And that includes a decent-sized sweetener for me, of course, so rock and roll over or the deal is dead as a dodo.

TRANSLATION: Roland, you better come through for me, you arsehole. I've fired the incumbent supplier, so you better make sure I get a decent price or else you are going to make me look a complete tit with our CEO. Fuck a win-win. I said that so you would be prepared to move. I want a far better price than this, and I don't give a monkey's if you win anything in this whole deal just as long as I get what I want.

47. BILLY BULLSHIT
GETS COLD-CALLED

TUESDAY 22ND AUGUST 4.24 PM

Let me stop you there, son. Look, I know where you are going with this call; heck, I will always be a step or two ahead of you. And everyone else, for that matter. Let me teach you some tricks of the trade from an award winner. Cold-calling is like aikido. It's not boxing; don't jab and weave. You have to use the customer's energy and redirect them to your killer throw. Lay an ambush, but elegantly lead them to it. You know what you did wrong? Let me tell you. You marched on with your script without realising that you have a human being on the end of the line. A human being, mind you, who occupies the C-suite. So, just bear that in mind. I am no ordinary desk jockey. I am the guy with the industry award, the press coverage and the corner office. Actually, I don't have a corner office as such. Never mind—the point is you need to know who you are dealing with. Do your research, understand the calibre of your target. Actually, let me tell you a story. I was in a client close the other day, and the sales staff were making a right hash of it, so yours truly stepped in to save the . . . hello? Are you there? Hello?

TRANSLATION: I have to do my part when amateurs and wannabe business development folk call me. I can see their game a mile away. Hey, good on them for trying. I mean, it's laughably bad, and I don't ever recall being so clumsy, but we all have to start somewhere. He will remember that call, that's for sure. This is the day when someone who cared taught him the tricks to success. Yeah, he was hanging off my every word. Good for him, too. Shame the line failed us . . .

TRIES SOCIAL SELLING

MONDAY 28TH AUGUST 3.00 PM

Exciting New Product Announcement

We at Toys R Fun are the world's sixth leading manufacturer of toys, and we have a new and exciting product to showcase. It's made from 100% synthetic organic polymers, with a high molecular mass. The QS9000 standards are rigorously adhered to during production, and our design team is highly skilled in Empathetic Creative Design. The new Urban Terror Wrist is the all-action toy for boys aged 7-11. Ergonomically designed to flexibly fit all wrist types and featuring a built-in replica Desert Eagle handgun, realistic serrated hunter knife and garrotte wire. Visit us today at www.urbanterrorwrist.com to learn more . . .

Comments:

Are you for fucking real? An ISIS starter kit? **@SirMikeAdams**

Does this new toy chop off kids fingers like the #croc-o-dial? **@mrsbamford**

First time on social media Billy? **@smoothercriminal**

Billy, how can it be both organic and synthetic? #notpossible **@Bob21**

This is a joke, right? **@RJD**

High molecular bullshit . . . **@EmmaTheal**

#worsttoyever **@TroyTools**

someone is getting fired soon **@blakiesing**

See all 4,396 comments

In response to you morons, toy manufacturing is a complex and precise endeavour. Not that any of you fuckwits would have a clue anyway. I suggest you get a higher dose of your medication and put your straitjackets on so that you can't use a computer. I am a respected (award winning) C-suiter who demands to be respected and revered in equal measure. The #terrorwrist is a genius idea and even better product. You dumb fucks just need to get a date in the diary for your lobotomies. And @mrsbamford you got your money back on the #croc-o-dial so just shut the fuck up @BillyBS

TRANSLATION: Who do these cheeky bastards think they are? I put out a perfectly acceptable announcement on social media and now I get a whole bunch of internet trolls taking the rise out of me. Fuckers. Who do they think they are messing with? I'm getting in amongst it. They won't know what's hit them by the time I have finished cyber-battering them. Talk about bringing a digital knife to a virtual reality gunfight.

49. BILLY BULLSHIT
CHATS TO THE CHAIRMAN

THURSDAY 7TH SEPTEMBER 2.13 PM

Mr. Johnson, actually it's great that we are sitting next to each other, as I wanted to bend your ear about the triple green metrics you instituted. Listen, I am not saying it needs a rework; after all, you can't unscramble scrambled eggs, right? But, by the same token, you can't make an omelette without breaking a few eggs either. And I think there are some broken silos that could be steadied and right-sided with some strategic intervention . . . led by, well, you know who. Patrick, can I call you Patrick? Ok, Mr. Johnson, let's be clear; I am not saying that these metrics are as useful as tits on a bull. I am just saying that we could square the circle a little bit, you know? Hey, listen, we could always do a soft launch of the Urban Terror Wrist and see how it flies?

Great to shoot the shit with you. I know you and I are singing from the same hymn sheet. Your silence says everything that I need to know from you, sir.

TRANSLATION: These triple green metrics are fucking terrible. No one gives two fucks about them, least of all me. If anything, they kind of expose that my department is lagging slightly, and I will be fucked if all my good work is going to come down to something so binary as these metrics. Fuck that.

50. BILLY BULLSHIT
AT A SEXUAL HARASSMENT HEARING

WEDNESDAY 13TH SEPTEMBER 9.07 AM

CHRO: Billy, these are very serious accusations being made against you and ones that we don't take lightly. We of course have to investigate these thoroughly, whether they are based on truth or purely accusatory. Please, let us hear from your perspective.

BB: Listen, I was merely trying to make Christina feel welcome. As the new receptionist, she needs to know who she can trust. It's a dog-eat-dog world in the corporate jungle, and I was merely trying to guide her through the bullpen and save her from the animals in sales. You know what they are like? Eh? Hunters, and she was their prey— sexually, I mean, if you didn't pick up on the analogy. Actually, it's hard for me to accept that I wasn't the hero in all of this.

CHRO: Erm, Billy, we are actually talking about a different person, Emily, in our graduate program . . . but please, go on. What's Christina got to do with this?

BB: Shit.

TRANSLATION: Oh, motherfucking Christ, I am in real shit now. Christina has landed me right in it. What a tart. And to think I had backed off her anyway. Jeez, try and help someone and be a bit friendly. Sure, I was flirty, but that's business, right?! I hope this is about Christina and not that young, perky creature in our grad program . . . what's her name? Emma. That's it. Seriously, me on a sexual harassment accusation? Everyone knows I love chicks. What a joke. Anyway, no one will ever believe that of me, so I'm pretty much bulletproof.

51. BILLY BULLSHIT
GETS FIRED

FRIDAY 22ND SEPTEMBER 6.02 PM

CEO: Billy, we need to have a word. Following your recent altercation with Client Services, the public rant on social media, the total financial disaster in Q3, the complete failure of the Croc-o-Dial product line and resultant compensation claims that may well cost the company millions, allowing the development of what can only be described as a toy for aspiring child members of Daesh, the sexual harassment charges levelled against you by now two members of staff, your puerile acceptance speech at the awards ceremony, your completely banal keynote speech at ToyCon '19, the totally inappropriate remarks you made at the LGBT council meeting, the utterly embarrassing comments you made when you met with the chairman recently, and a litany of many other faux pas, I am absolutely delighted to announce that you are fired. Effective immediately. And can I say, without fear of contradiction, you are the biggest bullshitter I have ever had the misfortune to work with.

BB: Fuck you.

TRANSLATION: Fuck you.

52. BILLY BULLSHIT
SPEAKS TO HIS FAMILY

FRIDAY 22ND SEPTEMBER 7.46 PM

My darling wife Jane Davies. My truly gifted children. My family. Daddy has some absolutely stellar news. I made a bold decision today for us, the inner circle. I have decided to let the desk knob jockeys . . . sorry, language . . . at work go screw themselves and continue their loser journey without me. Yep, that's right. I resigned, kicked them to the fucking kerb . . . sorry, language . . . re-sized myself into a new beginning. The truth is, guys, that your father is a leader and is not afraid to tell people where to stick it. So, moving forward, I will be home a bit more whilst I plan the next chapter of my career book. Such great news, hey, darling? Darling? Where are you going? Kids, why are you crying?

TRANSLATION: I got fired.

AUTHORS' ACKNOWLEDGMENTS

Jane Davies as Billy's long suffering wife. Tim Millard as Billy's long suffering boss.

We'd like to thank our illustrator, Kaitlynn Jolley.

Many of the phrases in this book were crowdsourced by using the LinkedIn community to tell us their most reviled bullshit words and business idioms.

With thanks to the following people who made a contribution to the book:

Judson Kinkade, Morgan Silver, Ron de Pear, Kristina Cleveland, Michelle Brown, Todd Williams, Gregory Carson, David Pearlstein, Christine Stevens, Trina West, Nicolas Thomson, Brooke Sagar, Sue Elms, David Louth, Amy James, Sarah Eichmann, Derek Akers, Deirdre Fryer, Steve Ryan, Tony Dunne, Agnes Vaysierre, Jessica Kern, John Deery-Schmitt, Justin Qubrosi, Carrie Mantey, Adrian Howe, Arthur Malone, Janine Palome, Jeremy Radford, Stuart Smith, Greg Simmons, Jessica Harrison, Fraser Bennie, Daniel Brown, Jerry Kurbatoff, Ian Gibbons,

Allyson Tessmann, Chris Torrence, Michael Donovan, Nilesh Rebello, Cara Robertson, Rodney Thompson, Jenny Arden, Alberto Palomino, Adrian Brown, Kevin Wincell, Lee Vecchione, Jake Evans, Megan F Kwee, Alex Demestihas, Aditee Lad, Lyle Knickrehm, Andrew Moravick, Carl Mueller, Brian Yacono, Arjun Singh, Matt Spencer, Josh Wood, Robert Curro, William Fetter, Oneil Franso, Michael Dolch, Kathy Gioia, David Issac, Kristina Cleveland, Joey Ben-Hail, Robert Newell, Graham Sharp, Ken Ossowicz, Gregory Wilson, Jen Van Deusen, Tony Dunne, Lori Boxer, Mike Gillkey, Victoria Weaver, Laura Waldusky, Andy Spigner, Michael Kinstad, Ben Emerson, Nicolas Thomson, Cristian W Potter, Jeremy Radford, Elliot Jones, Robert Curro, Joshua Abramson, Lawri Williamson, Pat Virnich, Mike Fretwell, Dave McCubbin, Justin Alexander, Terry Elgood, Amanda Roberson, Andrew Bailey, Beth Tarbell, Andrew Baber, Saj Zand-Lashani, George Fletcher, Joshua Smith, Jerry Cifra, Sabrina Benge, Donna Hughes, Jane Muxen McCullough, Patrick Lynch, Sharon Byrne, Jane Piper, Molly Tull, Kenneth Hamilton, Justin Purser, Tony Dunne, Michael Buzin, Nicolas Thomson, Jessica Kern, Caryn Gray, Stephanie Gatas, Craig Garbutt, Jason Whiteaker, Ryan Kane, Dane Mandato, Sarah Ball, Drew Prosperi, Derek Harding, Ali Bilal, Gabrielle Cahill, Tala Al Ansari, Phil Stone, Sherri Chien-Niclas, Lucy Webb, Michael Bacina, Chris Lazio, Paul Kazalski, Hugh Baldus, Nicolas Thomson, Michael Batres, Ronald S. Zarowitz, Stacey Riley, Caroline Trudeau, Sarah Albrecht, Joe Mayo-Cullen, Bill Meyer, Brad Brelo, Thomas Todd, Trish Chuipek, Linda Mellor, Mark Brown, Neil Sabey, Ryan Kane, Simon Hudson, Yury Magalif,

Joni Holderman, Wendy Likely, David McNamara, Ron Finklestein, Steve Glass, LaDanna James, Derek Mercer, Steven J. White, Richard Ledyard, Kevin Maier, Amy Soricelli, Colette Hogan, James Stein, Simon Foster, Brian Collins, Mike Miller, Marice Parchen, Crystal Swalens, Paul Snyderman, Dave Haydon, Kenneth Hamilton, Nicolas Thomson, Michael Cunningham, Maarten Albarda, Marko John Supronyuk, Jimmy Schnabel, Byron Sheffield, Shannon Sedgwick, Gary Barton, Vimal Mathew, Kelly Spiess, Greg Spraker, Barry Baxter, Sarvesh Singh, Michael Dolch, Mustafa Noaman Al-Qaisi, Brian Hathaway, Joshua Abramson, Barry Enderwick, Paul O'Sullivan, Stephen Stange, Mark Cunningham, Dave Henroid, Stuart Smith, Kristina Cleveland, Sophie Albrecht, Elaine Martin, Carrie Severson, Beth Tarbell, Allan Elliott, Paul Barnett, Tony Dunne, M. Robert Grunwald, Clinton Theil, Nathan King, Trevor Childs, Sue Elms, Nick McNeal, Edwin van Vulpen, Victoria Hayes, Paula Williams, Sara Fletcher, Drew Prosperi, Laragh Covington, Dave Haydon, Jen Van Deusen, Allen Larson, Linda Larsen, Benjamin Parker, Elaine Martin, Deborah Painter, Elijah Condellone, Marc Mulgrum, Amanda Tenedini, Nathan King, Ben Emerson, Niall Dunne, James Blair, Louis Houle, Beth Kludt, Candice Foster, Michel St-Germain, Marcus Grimm, Amy James, Rajesh D. Patel, David Slack, Tim Dodge, Donovan Craig, Peter J. Hurley, John Deery-Schmitt, Bill Crandall, Michael Gantly, Alex Arnold, Stuart Smith, Brittani Morgan, Mikhail Kuznetsov, Geoffrey Phillips, Paul Black, Robert Curro, Dakota Jacobsen, William Ferraiolo, Maree Northridge-Sugai, Megan F. Kwee, Michael Ottomanelli, Marla Topliff, Simon Fitzpatrick, Kevin Maier, Rudy

Sisto, Alan Mackenzie, Dave Purvis, Deb Wolniak, James Marable, Sandy Gonsalves, Thomas Hutton, David Crozier, Glenn Beckwith, Michael Waters, Darla Blackmore, Bill Reiss, Rachel Shields Williams, Ben Emerson, Andrew Williams, Shelley Summers, Byron Sheffield, Deborah Krug, Sabarni Palit, Martin Maxwell, Matthew Deutsch, Judd O'Toole, Issac Taylor, Joni Holderman, Jethro Cohen, Peter J. Hurley, Aaron Smith, Julian Ertelt, Alyssa Arnold, Ashley McKenna, Jessica Williamson, Dave Haydon, Dave Van Horn, Marci Sewell O'Neil, Neil Ifill, Shala Pelloni, Joni Holderman, Elaine Martin, Beth Davis-Olsen, Rachel Houghton, Janine Palome, Amanda Robertson, Elliot Jones, Stephanie Williams, Randall Stephens, Michele Klucar, Ben Emerson, Kristina Cleveland, Joni Holderman, Jessica Kern, Michael Dolch, Sophie Albrecht, Brian Friend, Rachel McCoy, Betsy Eklund, Jon Aiken, Dave Rubin, Wayne Cannel, Cory Whalin, Thomas J. Moore, Martin Barclay, Matthew Taylor, Becky Krumm, Arnis Venta, Andrew Barley, Craig Whittington, Steven Ford, Amy Bergman-Valla, Chris Haas, Shearin Dramby, Rafael Teles, Michael Bacina, Daphne van den Brule, Sarah Hall, Melanie Rivas, Carolyn Wilson, Allison Horan, Andrew Williams, Paul Snyderman, Rachel Shields Williams, Oneil Franso, Amy James, Byron Sheffield, Justin Purser, Jessica Kung, Kelly Spiess, Angela Siskey, Holly Johnson, William Ferraiolo, Jenell Rogers, Abbie Shuler, Joseph Towers, Aaron Lukken, Pam Skea, Sonya Pillay, Natalie Williams.

And thanks to the many thousands of other people who kindly offered their most hateful business phrases that didn't make it into this book but might make it into the next one . . .

ABOUT THE AUTHORS

Steve Blakeman—Writing has always been a passion of mine but has become an obsession over the past few years. I have used the LinkedIn Publishing platform to grow an audience and I now have over 300,000 Followers. I have been named as a 'Top 10 Writer on LinkedIn' for the past 4 years with articles that have been picked up and republished by the likes of Business Insider, Inc.com and Yahoo Finance plus quoted in books such as *The Digital Detectives*. The articles I write are regularly featured as Editor's Picks on LinkedIn and have had views as over a million for some pieces.

On the back of the LinkedIn accolade, I wrote 'How to be a Top 10 Writer on LinkedIn' which has sales/downloads of nearly 6000 copies since its launch in April 2016.

After 30+ years in advertising (an industry which thrives on a steady diet of BS and has more than its fair share of Billy's) I thought I had heard all the bullshit phrases that had ever been uttered. From the 'ask' to 'zero sum game' and all points in-between. However, after co-writing this book, I finally realised one thing—I had barely even seen the 'tip of the iceberg' . . .

 **Mike Adams**—My domain expertise lies in advising CEOs on how to scale and grow their business—I have clients all over the globe giving me exposure to a broad set of market and business conditions but also plenty of 'lingo' to draw from! I published a business book in 2015, *The Intrepid CEO— How Bold Leaders Future-proof Sales & Drive Profit—* which I crowd-funded and successfully reached the funding goal in the first day. This is a great platform to build from.

Additionally, I get to speak at conferences on business and sales adding to my brand position in market. As a consultant I am surrounded by peers using nonsensical, business rhetoric constantly . . . this book is a good self-effacing jibe.

CPSIA information can be obtained
at www.ICGtesting.com
Printed in the USA
BVHW031714160919
558568BV00001B/13/P